I0429202

Songs of the
EARTH

A TRIBUTE TO NATURE,
IN WORD AND IMAGE

Running Press
PHILADELPHIA · LONDON

Library of Congress Cataloging-in-Publication Number
94-67776

ISBN 1-56138-523-9

This book may be ordered by mail from the publisher.
Please add $1.00 for postage and handling.
But try your bookstore first!

Running Press Book Publishers
125 South Twenty-second Street
Philadelphia, Pennsylvania 19103-4399

INTRODUCTION

By viewing Nature, Nature's handmaid Art,
Makes mighty things from small beginnings grow.
—John Dryden

In the melodic whispers of the reeds, the graceful arc of a flower weighing the morning's dew, the brilliant kaleidoscope of a sunrise dazzling the landscape, and in so many other moments, nature has been a source of inspiration to mankind. Art

has become the way we have celebrated—and imitated—nature's beauty. Our music echoes the singing reeds, our dances mimic the swaying flowers, our paintings recreate the panorama of the landscape.

Within these pages are the voices of people and cultures from around the globe, in eras past and present, celebrating their relationship with the natural world. Like the many sounds of nature, their words have powerful, meaningful rhythms.

In the visions of these works you will find the wonders of nature, universal in effect and timeless in appeal.

I arise today

Through the strength of heaven:

Light of sun,

Radiance of moon,

Splendour of fire.

Speed of lightning,

Swiftness of wind,

Depth of sea,

Stability of earth,

Firmness of rock.

—Saint Patrick
5th-century Patron Saint of Ireland

. . . The first in time and the first in importance of the influences upon the mind is that of nature. Every day, the sun; and, after sunset, Night and her stars. Ever the winds blow; ever the grass grows. Every day, men and women, conversing —beholding and beholden.

—*Ralph Waldo Emerson (1803–1882)*
American writer and poet

Morning-fair, follow me further
back . . .

When the sun for me glinted the sides of
a sand grain,

and my intent stretched over the buds at
their first trembling.

—*Theodore Roethke (1908–1963)*
American poet

And bending across

the path as if saying prayers to welcome

the dawn, were long grasses which were

completely overpowered

by the thick dew.

—*Grace Ogot (b. 1930)*
Kenyan writer

When we get out of the glass bottles of
    our ego,

and when we escape like squirrels
    turning in the cages of
    our personality

and get into the forests again,

we shall shiver with cold and fright

but things will happen to us

so that we don't know ourselves.

Cool, unlying life will rush in,

and passion will make our bodies taut
 with power,

we shall stamp our feet with new power

and old things will fall down,

we shall laugh, and institutions will curl
 up like burnt paper.

—D.H. Lawrence (1885–1930)
English novelist

I feel

The link of nature draw me:
   flesh of flesh,

Bone of my bone thou art,
   and from thy state

Mine shall never be parted,
   bliss or woe.

—*John Milton (1608–1674)*
English poet

The faintness of the stars,

the freshness of the morning,

the dewdrop on the flower,

speaks to me.

—*Chief Dan George (1899–1981)*
Native American (Salish) logger, actor, and poet

The morning dawns

with an unwonted crimson;

the flowers more odorous seem;

the garden birds sing louder,

and the sun ascends the gaudy earth

with unusual brightness;

all nature smiles,

and the whole world is pleased.

—*Day Kellogg Lee (1816–1869)*
American theologian

Moonlight

is sculpture,

sunlight

is painting.

—*Nathaniel Hawthorne (1804–1864)*
American writer

The youth

of nature

is contagious. . . .

—*Edward Bulwer-Lytton (1803–1873)*
English novelist and politician

In beauty, I walk

To the direction of the rising sun

In beauty, I walk

To the direction traveling with the sun

In beauty, I walk

To the direction of the setting sun

In beauty, I walk . . .

All around me my land is beauty

In beauty, I walk

—*Navajo (Yebechi) chant*

Into the scented woods we'll go,
And see the blackthorn swim in snow.
High above, in the budding leaves,
A brooding dove awakes and grieves;
The glades with mingled music stir,
And wildly laughs the woodpecker.

—Mary Gladys Webb (1881–1927)
English novelist

I go to Nature

to be soothed

and healed,

and to have

my senses put

in tune once more.

—*John Burroughs (1837–1921)*
American naturalist

It is astonishing how many people cannot, or will not, hold still. I could not, or would not, hold still for thirty minutes inside, but at the creek I slow down, center down, empty . . . I retreat—not inside myself, but outside myself, so that I am a tissue of senses. Whatever I see is plenty, abundance. I am the skin of water the wind plays over; I am petal, feather, stone.

—*Annie Dillard (b. 1945)*
American writer

Here man is no longer the center of the world, only a witness, but a witness who is also a partner in the silent life of nature, bound by secret affinities to the trees.

—*Dag Hammarskjöld (1905–1961)*
Swedish diplomat and humanitarian

In the concert of nature

it is hard to keep

in tune with oneself

if one is out of tune

with everything else.

—*George Santayana (1863–1952)*
American poet and philosopher

Each of us needs to withdraw from the cares which will not withdraw from us. We need hours of aimless wandering or spates of time sitting on park benches, observing the mysterious world of ants and the canopy of treetops.

—*Maya Angelou (b. 1928)*
American writer and entertainer

Even such a happy Child of earth am I;

Even as these blissful creatures do I fare;

Far from the world I walk, and from
all care . . .

—*William Wordsworth (1770–1850)*
English poet

Surely there is something in the
unruffled calm of nature that overawes
our little anxieties and doubts: the sight
of the deep-blue sky, and the clustering
stars above, seem to impart a quiet
to the mind.

—Jonathan Edwards (1703–1758)
American theologian

We had the sky, up there, all speckled

with stars, and we used to lay on our

backs and look up at them, and discuss

about whether they was made, or only

just happened. . . .

—*Mark Twain (1835–1910)*
American humorist and writer

To those who have

not yet learned the

secret of true happiness,

begin now to study

the little things in

your own door yard.

—*George Washington Carver (c. 1864–1943)*
American botanist

[When] you walk along a country road and notice a little tuft of grass . . . the next time you pass that way you [must] stop to see how it is getting along and how much it has grown.

—*Georgia O'Keeffe (1887–1986)*
American painter

It is not the language of the painters but the language of nature to which one has to listen.

—*Vincent van Gogh (1853–1890)*
Dutch painter

. . . to the eyes of the man

of imagination

Nature is imagination itself.

As a man is, so he sees.

—*William Blake (1757–1827)*
English artist and poet

The subtlest

beauties in

our life

are unseen

and unheard.

—*Kahlil Gibran (1883–1931)*
Lebanese poet, novelist, essayist, and artist

Nature is not only what is visible to the eye—it shows the inner images of the soul—the images on the back side of the eyes.

—*Edvard Munch (1863–1944)*
Norwegian painter and printmaker

Nature is a foolish place to look for

inspiration in, but a charming one in

which to forget one ever had any.

—*Oscar Wilde (1854–1900)*
Irish poet and playwright

Sit in reverie, and watch the changing

color of the waves that break upon the

idle seashore of the mind.

—*Henry Wadsworth Longfellow (1807–1882)*
American poet

There is not a sprig of grass
that shoots uninteresting to me.

—*Thomas Jefferson (1743–1826)*
American president

The landscape is engorged with detail,

every movement of it chillingly sharp.

The air between people is charged. Days

unfold, bathed in their own music.

Nights become hallucinatory; dreams,

prescient.

—Gretel Ehrlich
20th-century American writer

. . . to listen to stars and birds, to babes and sages, with open heart. . . . This is to be my symphony.

—*William Henry Channing (1810–1884)*
American cleric

Down in the valley a couple of lions are roaring and the bull frogs are serenading, accompanied by the cicadas' finely tuned violins.

—*Bror Blixen (1886–1946)*
Swedish big-game hunter and socialite

I had no idea

nature made so much noise.

—*Richard Powers (b. 1957)*
American writer

Earth laughs in flowers.

—*Ralph Waldo Emerson (1803–1882)*
American writer and poet

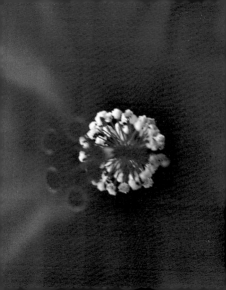

I lie on green bracken, amongst little yellow and magenta wild flowers whose names I don't know. I lie so close to the ground that my only view is of tall corn, so crisp that in the breeze it stirs with a noise like the rustle of silk.

—*Vita Sackville-West (1892–1962)*
English writer

Over the whole land

Spring thunders down in
		brilliant silence.

—*Ted Hughes (b. 1930)*
English poet

To linger silently among the healthful

woods, musing on such things as are

worthy of a wise and good man.

—*Horace (65–8 B.C.)*
Roman poet

We went and sat in a certain beech-wood

on a hill, a place of extraordinary beauty

looking like an early Gothic cathedral,

and with a glimpse of distant views in all

directions. The morning was fresh and

dewy, and I began to think that perhaps

there might be happiness in human life.

—*Bertrand Russell (1872–1970)*
English mathematician and philosopher

The everlasting universe of things

Flows through the mind, and rolls its

rapid wave.

—*Percy Bysshe Shelley (1792–1822)*
English poet

you ask
why I perch
on a jade green mountain?
I laugh
but say nothing
my heart
free
like a peach blossom
in the flowing stream
going by
in the depths
in another world
not among men

—Li Po (701–762)
Chinese poet

I do not know whether I was then a man

dreaming I was a butterfly, or whether I

am now a butterfly dreaming I am

a man.

—Chuang Tzu (369–286 B.C.)
Chinese sage

The butterfly flitting from flower to
flower ever remains mine,
I lose the one that is netted
by me.

—*Rabindranath Tagore (1861–1941)*
Indian poet

I once had a sparrow alight upon my

shoulder for a moment while I was hoe-

ing in a village garden, and I felt that I

was more distinguished by that circumstance than I should have been by any

epaulet I could have worn.

—*Henry David Thoreau (1817–1862)*
American writer

The dew brings thee jewels.

The winds bring perfume. . . .

The forest sings . . .

—*Henry Ward Beecher (1813–1887)*
American clergyman

What do the tall trees say
To the late havocs in the sky?
They sigh.
The air moves, and they sway.
When the breeze on the hill
Is still, then they stand still.
They wait.
They have no fear. Their fate
Is faith. Birdsong
Is all they've wanted, all along.

—*Wendell Berry (b. 1934)*
American poet, novelist, and essayist

I like trees because they seem more

resigned to the way they have to live

than other things do.

—*Willa Cather (1873–1947)*
American writer

The woods were made for the hunter
of dreams,
The brooks for the fishes of song.

—*Sam Walter Foss (1858–1911)*
American poet

. . . the banks are for the most part deep solitudes, overgrown with trees, which, hereabouts, are already in leaf and very green. For miles, and miles, and miles, these solitudes are unbroken by any sign of human life or trace of human footstep; nor is anything seen to move about them but the blue jay, whose color is so bright, and yet so delicate, that it looks like a flying flower.

—*Charles Dickens (1812–1870)*
English novelist

Land is also time. The greening of time is

a clock whose hands are blades of grass

moving vertically, up through the fringe

of numbers, spreading across the middle

of the face, sinking again as the sun moves

from one horizon to the other.

—*Gretel Ehrlich*
20th-century American writer

The corn grows up.

The waters of the dark clouds
    drop, drop.

The rain descends.

The waters from the corn leaves
    drop, drop.

The rain descends.

The waters from the plants drop, drop.

The corn grows up.

The waters of the dark mists drop, drop.

—*Washington Matthews*
19th-century Native American (Navajo) poet

I stopped to hike a trail into a

blackwater swamp of tupelo and bald

cypress. . . . I had this powerful sense of

life going about the business of getting

on with itself. . . . Things were growing

so fast I could almost feel the heat from

their generation: the slow friction of leaf

against bud case, petal against petal. For

some time I stood among the high

mysteries of being as they consumed the

decay of old life.

—*William Least Heat Moon*
20th-century American writer

Where, unwilling, dies the rose

Buds the new, another year.

—*Dorothy Parker (1893–1967)*
American writer

A child said *What is the grass?* fetching
　　　　it to one with full hands

How could I answer the child? I do not
　　　　know what it is any more
　　　　than he.

—*Walt Whitman (1819–1892)*
American poet

Nature imitates herself. A grain thrown into good ground brings forth fruit: a principle thrown into a good mind brings forth fruit. Everything is created and conducted by the same Master,—the root, the branch, the fruits,—the principles, the consequences.

—*Blaise Pascal (1623–1662)*
French mathematician and philosopher

Dunes like standing waves. Dunes like arcs and sickles, scythe blades and waning moons. Virgin dunes untracked by machines, untouched by human feet. Dunes firm and solid after rain, ribbed with ripple marks from the wind. Dunes surrounding ephemeral pools of water that glitter golden as tiger's eye in the light of dawn. . . . Sand and beauty. Sand and death. Sand and renewal.

—*Edward Abbey (1927–1989)*
American writer and park ranger

The sea quiet, shadow-colored and

without shadows.

From which shall rise

the sea wind, moving

swiftly towards the

steep jungles. The sea wind

the awakener.

ii

The sea wind is

a panther moving

swiftly towards the

mountain jungles.

Its silky fur

brushes me.

—*Denise Levertov (b. 1923)*
American poet

A generation goes, and a
        generation comes,
but the earth remains for ever.
The sun rises and the sun goes down,
and hastens to the place where it rises.
The wind blows to the south,
and goes round to the north;

round and round goes the wind,
and on its circuits the wind returns.
All streams run to the sea,
but the sea is not full;
to the place where the streams flow,
there they flow again.

—Ecclesiastes *1:4–7*

In her starry shade of dim and solitary

loveliness, I learn the language of

another world.

—*George Gordon, Lord Byron (1788–1824)*
English poet

The thing that makes the flowers open
and the snowflakes fall must contain a
wisdom and a final secret as intricate and
beautiful as the blooming camellia or the
clouds gathering above, so white and
pure in the blackness.

—*Anne Rice (b. 1941)*
American writer

Nature is often hidden,

sometimes overcome,

seldom extinguished.

—*Francis Bacon (1561–1626)*
English philosopher

There on the flat stone, on which we so often have sat to weep and pray, we look down, and see it covered with the fossil footprints of great birds and the beautiful skeleton of a fish. We have so often tried to picture in our mind what the fossilized remains of creatures must be like, and all

the while we sat on them. We have been

so blinded by thinking and feeling that

we have never seen the world.

—Olive Schreiner (1855–1920)
South African writer and feminist

Among the scenes which are deeply impressed on my mind, none exceed in sublimity the primeval forests undefaced by the hand of man . . . no one can stand in these solitudes unmoved, and not feel that there is more in man than the mere breath of his body.

—*Charles Darwin (1809–1882)*
English naturalist

In the skin of our fingers

we can see the trail of the wind;

it shows us where the wind blew

when our ancestors were created.

—*Native American (Navajo) legend*

We are like butterflies who flutter for a day and think it is forever.

—*Carl Sagan*
20th-century American writer

Wild bird singer, sing on!

Nothing lives long
But the earth and the mountain
What remains in the fire, in the flames
Becomes the final song

Listen hard to the words
From the winter's whiteness they come
And on this day too old to run am I
Too old for the land of the young

Black Kettle raises the flag

The air is crisp and cold

Here at my home I sing

Nothing lives long

But the earth and the mountain

White Antelope is my name

—*Charles Ballard*
20th-century Native American
(Quapaw/Cherokee) poet

Whatever befalls the earth

befalls the sons and daughters of
the earth.

We did not weave the web of life;

We are merely a strand in it.

Whatever we do to the web,

we do to ourselves. . . .

—*Chief Seattle (1788–1866)*
Native American (Suquamish) leader

Turn away no more:

Why wilt thou turn away

The starry floor

The watry shore

Is giv'n thee till the break of day.

—William Blake (1757–1827)
English artist and poet

. . . For I have learned

To look on nature, not as in the hour

Of thoughtless youth, but hearing
     oftentimes

The still, sad music of humanity. . . .

—*William Wordsworth (1770–1850)*
English poet

Since the whole world

Cannot buy

A single spring day,

Of what avail

To seek yellow gold?

—Hsi Pei Lan
Ch'ing Dynasty poet

LAND

Without this
what is
worth doing.

—*Carroll Arnett (b. 1927)*
Native American (Cherokee) poet

One touch

of nature

makes

the whole world kin.

—William Shakespeare (1564–1616)
English dramatist and poet

Unknown to me what resideth
here
Tears flow from a sense of unworthiness
and gratitude.

—*Anonymous Japanese poet*

Soil for legs

Axe for hands

Flower for eyes

Bird for ears

Mushroom for nose

Smile for mouth

Songs for lungs

Sweat for skin

Wind for mind

—Nanao Sakaki
20th-century Japanese poet

Sunsets and rainbows, green forest and
restive blue seas, all

naturally colored things are my siblings.
We have played

together on the floor of the world

Since the first stone looked up

At the stars.

—*Maya Angelou (b. 1928)*
American writer and entertainer

The rainbow raised up with me.

Through the middle of broad fields,

The rainbow returned with me.

To where my house is visible,

The rainbow returned to me.

—*Native American (Navajo) poem*

Every bird song, wind song, and tremendous storm song of the rocks in the heart of the mountains is our song, our very own, and sings our love.

—John Muir (1838–1914)
American naturalist

And forget not that the earth delights to feel your bare feet and the winds long to play with your hair.

—*Kahlil Gibran (1883–1931)*
Lebanese poet, novelist, essayist, and artist

Remember that you

are this universe

and this universe

is you.

—*Joy Harjo (b. 1951)*
Native American (Creek) writer

. . . from the stars

and the sun

and the moon

should man learn.

—*Eagle Chief (Letakots-Lesa)*
20th-century Native American (Pawnee) leader

Silently one by one, in the infinite
meadows of heaven

Blossomed the lovely stars, the
forget-me-nots of the angels.

—*Henry Wadsworth Longfellow (1807–1882)*
American poet

Come out of your warm, angular house,

resounding with few voices, into the chill,

grand, instantaneous night, with such a

Presence as a full moon in the clouds, and

you are struck with poetic wonder.

—*Ralph Waldo Emerson (1803–1882)*
American essayist and poet

When the great earth, abandoning day, rolls up the deeps of the heavens and the universe, a new door opens for the human spirit. . . . For a moment of night we have a glimpse of ourselves and of our world islanded in its stream of stars—pilgrims of mortality, voyaging between horizons across eternal seas of space and time.

—Henry Beston (1888–1968)
American writer and naturalist

I only went out for a walk

and finally concluded to stay out

until sundown,

for going out,

I found,

was really going in.

—*John Muir (1838–1914)*
American naturalist

ACKNOWLEDGMENTS

TEXT

P. 8: "Saint Patrick" from *Celtic Christianity*, Lindisfarne Press, copyright © 1987; pp. 14–15: "Escape" by D.H. Lawrence, from *The Complete Works of D.H. Lawrence* by D.H. Lawrence, edited by V. de Sola Pinto & F.W. Roberts. Copyright © 1964, 1971 by Angelo Ravagli and C.M. Weekley, Executors of the Estate of Frieda Lawrence Ravagli. Used by permission of Viking Penguin, a division of Penguin Books USA Inc., and Laurence Pollinger Ltd. and the Estate of Frieda Lawrence Ravagli; p. 23: "Green Rain" from *Poems and the Spring of Joy* by Mary Webb, published by Jonathan Cape and reprinted by permission of the Estate of the Author; p. 54: "Spring Nature Notes," from *Season Songs* by Ted Hughes. Copyright © 1968, 1973, 1975 by Ted Hughes. Reprinted by permission of Viking Penguin, a division of Penguin Books USA Inc. and by permission of Faber and Faber Ltd.; p. 60: "On the mountain: A conversation" by Li Po, from *Bright Moon, Perching Bird*, copyright © 1987 by J.P. Seaton and James M. Cryer. Translation by James M. Cryer; pp. 64–65: "Hummingbird" by Harold Littlebird, copyright © 1975 by Kenneth Rosen. Reprinted from *Voices of the Rainbow* edited by Kenneth Rosen, published by Seaver Books, New York, New York; p. 67: Reprinted with permission of Simon & Schuster from *Fireflies* by Rabindranath Tagore. Copyright © 1928 by Macmillan Publishing Company, renewed 1955 by Rabindranath Tagore; p. 71: "What do the tall trees say?" by Wendell Berry, from *Sabbaths* 1991. Reprinted by permission of Wendell Berry; p. 80: "Recurrence," from *The Portable Dorothy Parker* by Dorothy Parker, Introduction by Brendan Gill. Copyright © 1928, renewed © 1956

ART

PP. 6, 9, 20, 24, 42, 61, 91, 96, 109, 114: by Ansel Adams, National Archives and Records Administration; pp. 12–13, 29, 36–37, 51, 52, 73, 81, 84, 116–117: Copyright © 1995 Julius Friedman; pp. 30, 49, 59, 103, 120: Illustrations by Frank McShane; pp. 1, 74–75, 94–95, 107: Courtesy of Letraset USA.

This book has been bound using handcraft methods, and Smyth-sewn to ensure durability.

The dust jacket and interior were designed by Christian Benton.

The cover was illustrated by Letraset.

The text was edited by Virginia Mattingly.

The text was set in Adobe Garamond by Deborah Lugar.

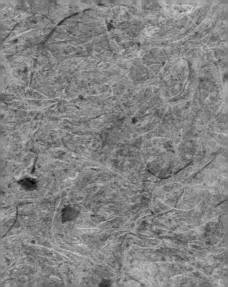